A DREAM AND THE SONG OF CŒDMON.

A DREAM

AND

THE SONG OF CŒDMON.

(A LEGEND OF WHITBY.)

BY J. M. J.

LONDON:

GEORGE BELL AND SONS, YORK STREET,

COVENT GARDEN.

1875.

CHISWICK PRESS :—PRINTED BY WHITTINGHAM AND WILKINS,
TOOKS COURT, CHANCERY LANE.

A DREAM.

PRELUDE.

THE sea lay calm and still,—a sultry
  breath
Of noontide sun had o'er it crept, and
  brooded
In trembling mirage on its waveless way.—
Spirit-entranced it slept ;—no ripple curved
The dark green shadow.—Outflowing, restless tide
Just stirr'd the water with its buoyant throb
Like the sweet heaving of a baby's breast
In dreamland.
    Through the quivering firmament
Piles of mist-fleeces gather'd up their folds
In changeful imagery, wakening as they moved
Sweet chords of colour, saffron, red, and blue,—
Not the dark liquid blue of eastern sapphire,

But the veil'd tenderness of turquoise tint,
Fading in northern climes ;—until anon
The shadows gather'd strength 'midst gorgeous
          tones
Of ruby purple on to ruby gold.—
Slowly the sinking sun made haste to dip
Beneath the boundless sea—infinite through
Its dim uncertain ending ;—high it hung
'Mid the thin mist, like pale, translucent star,
Rather than wearing the eye-dazzling glare
Of daylight's molten orb:—but far away,
Up high and high, the tiny cloudlet groups,
Like waiting sentinels in close array,
Wreathed their swift-changing filaments of gold
Around the setting sun.—The land-lock'd coast
In winding bays crept round the quiet shore,
And earth and heaven, blent in blaze of light,
Seem'd one.—

      Who hath not felt a sudden thrill
With speed of lightning flash across the mind
As some stray tone awakens up the past,
Whirling in fitful eddies the sear'd leaves
Of bygone days ?—Thus floated on my ear
The soft low-measured dash of well-timed oar,

With drooping breeze startling the voiceless sea,—
Youth's hours of pleasance, when the passing
    clouds
Were rainbow'd.—Down the broken pathway grey,
Down to the far shore winding, I bent my steps,
And, rousing from his dreams an aged mate
Of many angling pastimes, soon we launch'd
His tiny craft upon the mirror'd sea,
Each oar-stroke, bounding back, its note of speed,
Contending with the silence, till she lay
At pleasure anchor'd on the mimic waves
Tunefully lapping 'neath the buoyant keel.

The wooing tenderness—the hallow'd calm
Roused not keen longing for the angler's chance,
But sooner weaved a spell about the heart
Of sweet repose; old slumbering harmonies
Rhymed in with wandering thoughts; melodious
      wavelets
Rising or falling in their mystic song
In many-toned vibrations, as the chord
Snaps of a hidden, long-forgotten lyre,
The sweetest tone breathes lingering in the sound
That swells ere dying on the ambient air,

So with lost memories.   They throng and throng,
Quickening the heart's intensity of thought,
Until one image, fairer than the rest,
Outshines the paler ones, and we give heed
To its sole whisper.   Changeful thus in mood,
Gladly I yielded all the promised sport
Unto my willing mate, and thus at large
Upon the oar-bench laid me down to watch
The fleeting brilliance of the scene around.

The sacred pile of Hilda, hoar with age,
Crown'd the steep summit of the rocky shore
Skirting the far green-deep.   Not then it look'd
Grey with the count of ages ; sooner far
Bright as mosaic of old Rome, all wrought
With quaint device and curious workmanship.
The old walls, fringed with tufts of slender grass,
Glow'd midst the blue-grey ether ; trailing plants
Twisted their fibres round the broken arch
Or through the storm-rent gap ; yellow lichens
The carved stones enamell'd ;—sharp and cold
Their pencill'd tracery, contrasting well
With the bright blazing gold upon their patches
The scarr'd cliff's riven sides, which Titan-like

Had waged fierce battle with the tides of ages,
Wore the green livery of the bitter wave
Rolling around their base ; while peering through
The shale seem'd layers of malachite long buried.
But down, far down, on the low shelving beach
Deep shadow-shrouded headlands, bays, and
    tumbling
Landslips ; one vast and formless mystery,
Like an old man wearied with lapse of years,
Scant silver hair, and lustre-lacking eye,
Standing upon his Pisgah, looketh back
Upon the road by which he clomb, and sees
Only dim outlines, fading memories
Of the life pass'd.
           Yet I recall the day
When the dread storm-fiend, poised on wings of
    death,
Shrouded that mighty pile in night's dark gloom.
Above, around, the shrill wind hissing rent
The ebon clouds, and whirl'd white sheets of rain
Down on the angry sea, which toss'd aloft
The yeasty waters on the broken shore
In thundering avalanch.   Dead centuries
Of restless waves had chisell'd out dark caves

                      A Dream.

Through tall fantastic pillars, whence echoes came
Curdling the blood with fear.   Back from these homes,
       homes,
Back rush'd the fretted flood with deafening noise,
Scattering in flakes of foam its shiver'd spray
On the next curling wave, as it uprose
With sullen roar and gather'd strength, again
To dash its surf upon the wreck-strewn strand.

   What hoary Joliïm of a shadowy past
Lay crouch'd with wreathed brow of monarch, mid
Those solitudes ? A foe to grapple with,
And thrust from sanctuary and home of ages ?
The giants of the deep had won the day,
And toss'd their madden'd surges, till the joints
Of his vast dome lay shatter'd to a heap
Of dizzy ruins, and beneath he lay,
The wind among the hollows making moan
As of a dirge or requiem of the dead.

   Low lines of roofs, spread out in sun and shade
With glittering spires, their many angles dimm'd
Through the grey film of smoke.   The lawn look'd dwarf'd
       look'd dwarf'd
Beneath the ruin'd pile link'd round by years

Of gather'd memories.   Yet sympathy
For what is great and good, for noble deeds
That soothe the spirit or exalt the soul,
The nimbus which enwreathes its halo round
The mystic past, hath root within the heart
To-day as yesterday; lives in the hum
Of busy toil that girdles all the earth;
Lives in the strength that sways the brawny limb
Whose toilsome labour has no other bent
Than hammering out man's coil of daily wants;
Lives in the pinched frame, whose pallid cheek
Flushes through the winnowing of the spirit's
        wings,
Whispering " Thy Will be done."

                              How often sad
And dire mischance, as with a whirlwind's force
Drifts out the sands of human life, and death
Gathers his victims from the trembling throng.
But stands there one among them with a soul
Loyal to self—with nerves to his bidding calm—
He counts among the great ones of the earth,
And dies a hero, grappling with his foe.
Hope's winged meteor sinks in the abyss
Upon whose verge he stands, but far above

The mourning wail of death floats up, the last
Love-laden whisper of a lost life's song.—
Blotted the name from life's brief calendar,
But not the deed,—for, resting o'er the grave
Of frail humanity, undying, beams
The fadeless glory of heroic worth.
Eyes red with tears upraise their heavy lids
To gaze upon that after-glow, whose light
Gives healing, as the incense fragrance sweet
Such as the trailing, trembling woodbine sheds,
When the cool night has buried burning day.

Yet few from out those serried ranks of toilers
Win either glory or the martyr's crown.
The ploughshare of affliction furrows deep;
Voiceless its passing.   Scant the whiten'd locks;
Wither'd the lips; words have not weight to
            breathe
The soul's lament; spirit unto spirit sighs
Sadly "I mourn."   And solace slowly comes
With higher faith, the heritage and seal
Of man's divinity.   Thus the same stroke
Furrows and fructifies the heart, and will
More reverently turns to scan the work

Here to complete, with higher, nobler thoughts
And energy; as if the human stem
Lack'd vital power to bear a double bloom;
One withers, droops, and dies; and straight the
     petals
Of the other quick expand, and doubly grow
Through double nurture.
                If a thought could die,
Or be matured and compass'd by one mind,
One life might gauge its meaning, and the germ
Of foregone thought, garner'd for future time,
Would not exist; but being vital now
Through manifold suggestions, far beyond
The limit of a life, it cannot die.
Each rising generation holds the clue
For further quest. Erratic in its growth,
Up as a winged seed it comes to life,
In most strange places, bearing fruit according
To the soil it falls on. Epochs pass and pass;
To the gathering heir-loom each its quota yields,
And writes its sequence down on history's rolls,
From whence Time marshals up his noble peers,
Around whose names bright burns the Phœnix
     flame

Of immortality.   Suns of the past!
Ye shed your effluence on the age that is,
Which with in-added strength will cast its gains
To float on the unknown mysterious future.

   Thus musing on the graces that give life
A zest and meaning, 'midst the numberless
Unquiet dreams that dim its wayfaring,
Like flitting shadows dappling all the sunshine,
Methought the silver chimes of the spent hour
Greeted my ear; and then I seem'd to stand
Within the precincts of that holy fane.
Twilight had cast its glamour on the scene,
The stars shone here and there with fitful glance,
Low had the young moon dropp'd her silver bow,
Paling the shadows with faint streaks of light.
The hum of beetle or of insect wing,
The whirr of night-moth, hovering for its mate,
The pendent ivy's tremulous loose spray
Just shimmering in the moonlight, and the lap
Of ebbing tide, sweeping the shingly beach,
These sounds join'd harmony with the still night's
Mysterious voice, and kept her as from sleep
While she crept onward with her noiseless tread.

With all my senses closely knit to taste
This soften'd loveliness, this solemn hush
In the world's roundelay, something disturb'd
The quietude in which I lay entranced.
Within the archway doubtful gleam'd a light,
Like a thin mist, that clove the yielding air,
Till with bright rays, from sunlit clouds confused,
It took a brighter glory; when I traced
A band of shadowy figures carrying scrolls
Borne on the misty cloud.   One, than the rest
More noble, like a seer of bygone race,
With deep prophetic eyes, so heavenly calm,
Advanced to where I stood.   The ebbing blood
Moved not my feeble limbs, for all the pulses
Of life seem'd stay'd at once, and 'gainst a pillar
I lean'd for shelter, till the mind cast off
The icy hands of craven fear.   Then up
I look'd, and saw Cœdmon of Stronesleigh,
The Saxon bard.

           As something dim'd my sight
With sudden start, a voice behind me said,
" The tide is ebbing, sir; shall we lift anchor ? "
Then was it all a dream ? My meteor poet
A drifting scene of half-awaking sleep,

Rendering most palpable the subtle-wing'd
False fantasies of thought ?

               " Yes, let us haste
To regain the shore."   So, paddling homeward
     straight,
Gladly the oar I took, musing the while
On the weird mystery of changeful dreams,
With the mind's bias on the wakeful heart;—
Until I made resolve to search old rhymes
Wherein the song of Cœdmon's teaching lay,
Full of the pathos of a simple faith
Ingrain'd with truth, and reverent earnestness
For things divine ; with child-like worshipping
Of nature's secrets all received on trust ;—
For, being past their scan, with homage due,
God-like they held them, as coming straight from
     God.

THE SONG OF CŒDMON.

CŒDMON, of Eskdale, with its winding
    stream
    Slow trailing on through Whitby's busy
      haunts,
Crown'd with rare loveliness of hill and dale,
Sweet honey-scented breeze from purple ling,
Or freshening from the sea; at earlier date
But a wild stray of posied woods, and soft
Green sloping banks, with shadows dipping
    through
Its lucid stream; no stir of life, saving
Wild scream of ern, or ringed diver's splash,
Breaking upon the stillness ;—
                Churl he was,
Doing his master's bidding, or perforce

The thraldom of a hind burden'd his life
With service.   (Since the life we render here
Is one of service, what imports the sign
Under the which we toil, the badge we wear?
The question is, walk we with love's great light
About our path, or is the way obscured,
Dimm'd, by the ever-growing shade of self?)
Strange in his bearing, shy and grave, he lived
Companionless among his fellow-men;
Though not unloved.   Beneath his ample brow
Beam'd forth kind, lustrous eyes, with look
  brimful
Of pity, gazing tenderly upon
The world, with its swift many-sided ways.

Where the receding tide had stranded high
Upon the beach but broken limpet shells
And tangled weed—where the silvery bar
'Gainst the blue sky seem'd the sole girdling
  charm,
Holding the sea back,—dreamingly he gazed
On what seem'd vacancy to common eye;
Or, when the greedy sea, most miser-like,
Return'd with clouds of spray, and swept amid

The curling waves scatt'rings of many tides,
Some mandate thrall'd his spirit, heard from out
The tossing fray of mingled elements.
Across the harbour's flow, where the ships' masts
Crowd thickest, and the mighty shore-ridge grand
Climbs heavenwards, one greatcliffoutwardbending
With such, stretch seaward, ever dips its base
Into the depthless bosom of the sea.
Sometimes 'twixt passing cloud the sun would shed
On the grey lias dancing streams of light,
Flooding adown its rugged edge and seams
Like rippling silver ; but it mostly stood
A darken'd pile, fit outpost first to greet
The rising tide with thunders of salute ;
Then the torn yellow foam whirl'd in and out
Its shatter'd sides, tossing with booming crash
The boiling eddies.   There would Cœdmon sit
Like carven rock, watching the waters toil,
Or the outstretch'd immensity of space.
Deed fraught with ill, or ought that could have
          marr'd
The frailest beauty of created things,
Ne'er had his pleasure been ; for sympathy
With whatsoe'er held vital force from God

Found in his heart response.   Such natures live
Sustain'd and purified by Hebe draughts
Flowing to their lips measureless and pure
Through the long feverish span of toilsome day.
Gently fell footsteps his wayfaring through,
Fearful lest this same lonesomeness of mood
That warp'd his seeming, should to others show
Lack of regard, giving sharp sting of pain
From narrow selfishness, clogging his path
With noisome weeds.   Thus then he lived apart,
Like some lone visionary ; outer life
Had neither ebb nor flow ; a hidden mere
Sleeping in hollows, with no babbling brook
For outlet, and when rack'd with sudden storms
The echoes sent reverberating tones
Back only to its own lone silent shores.

    It was the age of rhyme and song.   Great deeds
Were told in Sagas, ancient histories
Of precious memory.   On festivals
And days of victory, the song went round,
And he who could not join the glee or strike
The harp was a sure scorn of men, a carl !

A base-born knave, worthy of flippant scoff
And cold neglect.   Now Cœdmon could not sing.
No words from craving heart found utterance ;
Their very wealth served but to block the flow,
The outlet of his thoughts.   A shifting whirl
Of multiform ideas floated round
Like phantasies from sick, unhealthy brain,
Darken'd his path the shadow of his mind,
Filling him with a look of restless pain,
With deepening furrows, as from dried-up tears.
So, like a wounded hart, he shelter sought
In lonely covert, where the sweeping rush
Of his co-mates, through purple heather bounding
And golden fern, could never reach his ear ;
There he lay hidden, ever moaning forth
The burden of his life, " I cannot sing."

One day at Yule-tide there was banquet given.
Cœdmon was bidden guest, his friend the Reeve
Giving great welcome in the banner'd hall.
Right merry was the cheer, laden the board
With well-fill'd platters, and small stint of mead.
Blithe were the folk, chatt'ring of this and that
With much quaint humour.   Flashes of keen wit

Breaking with laughter through the buzz of words
As the feast lengthen'd; then the wassail cup
Pass'd freely round; anon a cry broke forth,
" Bring out the harp, the merry harp, that each
May sing in turn the song he loves the best."

One rose to take it, bronzed with briny breeze
From the green dancing waves; a Viking bold
He look'd; his clear keen eye bright with the
  glow
Of ready purpose; rough and massive hands,
Well used to handle rope and oar, were his
At best.   Deftly he touch'd the strings
While with full voice and measure gay he sang:

THE LANDING OF THE SAXONS.

Hurrah ! The sea, the sea !
 Our ocean-steed !
Riding so gallantly
 With winged speed ;

Dashing through yellow foam
 And glittering spray,
The wild sea is our home,
 And free highway.

Hurrah ! the bonny sea,
  With crested wave ;
May its broad bosom be
  Our home or grave.

From Jutland o'er the main
  The long ships ride ;
Hengist and Horsa came
  Thus side by side.

Upon the yellow sand
  Of Britain's shore,
The valiant Vikings stand
  Ready for war.

" What is thy scott and gift,
  King of the Isle,
If we our saxes lift
  To rid awhile

Thee of thy northern foes ? "
  (For since the day
The Romans left, but woes,
  The people say,

Have been their heritage ;)
   " Ay, willingly
If thou wilt give me gage
   I will give fee,

And Udal right for aye
   Of Thanet's isle."
The Norsemen sail away,
   Their keels the while

Whiten the tossing waves,
   The sea-gulls scream
Around the rock-ribb'd caves,
   As the oars gleam

Athwart the bounding sea.
   They gain the strand;
Furling the sails with glee
   They jump on land.

What boots it me to tell
   How every blow
That from their axes fell
   Laid down a foe;

Or how the clang of shield,
  The heavy stroke
Of the blue swords they wield
  The silence broke?

Enough it is to say,
  These North-men bold
Were driven far away
  Among the cold

Blue mists of their own hills;
  And thus they freed
The land from Pictish ills
  By this brave deed.

Soon for this sea-girt isle
  Made they just claim,
And this is how erewhile
  We Saxons came.

Who is it rises now with mien so proud,
And eyes so full of sadness?   Days long since
As kings his ancestors held rule within
The land, and now were waken'd bitter thoughts
By the gay seaman's song.   Awhile the harp
He held till the mood pass'd, then chanting sang:

Boadicea.

I see a vision, mistily arising,
Fillet-bound tresses, eyelids sorrow-laden,
From winged chariot high aloft she flings her
     Arms, shrieking, War! War!

Blood is our cup now, violence our portion;
Banish'd is freedom, since the Roman banner
Tainted the free breeze of the Icenian shore-lands;
     Vengers of Britain,

Rise with swords furbish'd, or to win or perish;
'Gainst the foe let bare breasts make iron
   ramparts;
Oh, shame! flash forth your crimson fire on
   coward's
     Cheek, till they cry, War.

Sad, oh! sad, are these evil days we live in;
Gold cannot hide the deep hurt of my people,
Wringing of hands gold cannot stay, nor hide
   black
     Stains of dishonour.

Hear ye not weeping? Wailing slow from mothers'
Hearts, mourning homes now desolate; the cry
    goes
Out on the wind's wings, far and near, the land
    through,
        Clamouring, War, War!

Fair were my loved ones in their youth's fresh
    Maytime,
Voices like sighings of the west-wind theirs—souls
Dew-pure.   With low plaint from white lips scarce
    parted,
        Trembling with anguish,

Hands lightly grasp'd o'er sorrow-sunken faces,
Plead they for vengeance swept on cruel spoilers,
By loving memories of sweet days past clinging
        Tendril-like round us.

Full of endearments sweet, of life unutter'd,
Full of the young heart's melody out-yearning
For loving joys that bloody hands have reft them.
        By holy longings,

Feeble words floating all our woes to heaven,
Trembling with hate and passionate entreaty,
Girt with rent robes, and loose unwoven tresses,
       Plead we for vengeance.

Britons! unloosed must soon be war's fierce
    bloodhounds,
Making the murky air with horror laden;
Up! Let not mercy blunt the bitter sword-edge,
       But cry on, War! War!

Now was it held by one of different mould;
He pass'd his long thin hand across the strings;
Eolian tones from ductile fingers flow'd;
With passion stirr'd, the eye dilated bright
As the sweet jingling harmonies came forth
In answer to his touch, and with hush'd voice,
Rich in melodious cadence, softly sang:

THE SUPREMACY OF LOVE.

I sing of love! Is there a warrior's gift
  Can vie with the bright burning gold
That rests upon thy wings, when thou dost sit
  Brooding, and to thy breast dost fold

Records and names on which thy pen hath writ
  "Holy?" He is a thrall would hold
The golden ransom more than a loved life,
  Or with foul taint would smirch thy name,
Sweet Spirit! Flowers of immortal type
  Entwine thy brow, bright as a flame;
No glory's token of a mortal strife,
  Or wreathèd coronal of fame,
But choicest seeds from heaven have set them
      there,
And nothing else on earth so sweet, so fair.

Oh! lead me ever on through life, with eyes
  Glistening with softest drops of balm
From the pure love that deep within them lies,
  With words thrilling—as if a psalm
Had drifted in sweet echoes from the skies;
  So shall my days be bless'd and calm.
Or should it be that they were full of ruth,
  And I and hope must be forsworn,
Still in the saddest hour thy bright glad truth
  Would rift across the darkest storm.
And better thus to see thee than, forsooth,
  For thy sweet presence ever mourn;

So let me see thee in the sorrow given,
And trust thy light to lead me on to heaven.

Came one in turn whose laughter-loving eyes
And ruddy cheek told he had lived to see
The sparkle on life's wave, but not the cloud
That darken'd it.   With jest and jaunty air
He twang'd the chord, and sang in sportive mood

ROWENA.

While earth is fair and gay,
        And the sun shines,
Mirth will not flee away,
        Although at times
Laughter will ripple low,
As if it were so so ;
Well, then, just let him go.

He will come back again,
        The merry lout,
With quirks of hearty strain,
        And full soon scout
All threats of sighs and tears,
All mutterings of fears,
For untold future years.

Now if there be a time
        When folks are gay
(This knowledge is not mine),
        It is, they say,
When some fair maiden slight
Hath sorely blear'd the sight
Of an unlucky wight

Who nought but her can see,
        And lives on sighs.
However bad she be
        For her he dies.
This sure was just the state
Of Vortigern, who sate
All joyous and elate,

Guest to his Saxon host.
        Rowena came
And gave her loyal toast;
        And, lo ! the flame
Kindled within his breast,
Nor had he peace or rest
Until he gain'd his quest.

" Health to my lord the king,"
        She kneeling said.
" What doth the maiden sing ? "
        (He was not read
In Saxon tongue.)   " Thy weal
She drinks as she doth kneel,
Say thou 'Drinc heal ! ' "

The wassail cup he took
        And pledged her so ;
And thus her winning look
        Brought heavy woe
Down on the British race ;
Pass'd was her day of grace,
And troubles grew apace.

But to the wassail cup .
        Let us all drink,
Every one standing up
        Fill to the brink ;
Fill to the wassail cup !
Hail to the wassail cup !
Long live the wassail cup

Then many voices urged on Ellerman
To sing a dirge well known of other days.
With quick assent he took the proffer'd harp
And swept his wrinkled hand with vigorous
    touch
Across the strings ; forth came a monotone
Of sadness, like the moan of driving storm
Through wither'd branches, and the rest upstood
To echo back its dying burden thus.
With bended head, his grey beard flowing down
Unto his girdle, slowly did he chant

THE BURNING OF THE SEA KING.

Hush'd is the clash of sword-blades, hush'd the
    sound ;
Haki, of many fights, lies on the ground,
Deep was the sword-thrust given, deep the
    wound,
        Deep was the wound.

He lifted up his battle-axe on high ;
Lo ! from his grasp it fell.   Then rose the cry,
" Lay me within my keel, that I may die,
        That I may die."

Weeping his warriors round about him stand
And raise him tenderly, hand lock'd to hand,
Gently they bore him down unto the strand,
          Unto the strand.

The Sea-hawk that had rode through many a gale,
With ebon beak for prow, and gilded tail,
Drew they to shore, hoisting the wingèd sail,
          The wingèd sail.

High on the deck with hasty hands they rear
A pile of slaughter'd foes, and warlike gear,
The dinted buckler and the broken spear,
          The broken spear.

Whilst in low tones Odin's death song they sing,
Wrapp'd in his runic robe, and mystic ring,
Sadly on deck they laid their loved sea-king,
          Their loved sea-king.

With failing eye he turn'd his head and scann'd
The Vicks and Fiords of his own native land ;
But passionless and cold lay that strong hand,
          Lay that strong hand.

The grand old face, with silver beard and hair,
Sear'd by the wind, fell pale upon his bier,
While frenzy lit his eye with dying flare,
>> With dying flare.

The pile they lighted; and the crackling wood
In clear-red flame whizzing above the flood,
The wingèd thing broke loose from where she stood,
>> From where she stood.

Her oaken-keel in a white furrow lay,
As in a whirling flame she sail'd away
With our old noble king.   Alack the day,
>> Alack the day!

Awhile the white smoke curl'd then wreathing high,
It floated on until it touch'd the sky.
So did he pass away.   So did he die,
>> So did he die!

King Haki's voice is in the ocean's roar
Bounding for ever back from shore to shore;
But his great war-cry hath been heard no more,
>> No more, no more!

Alas ! the harp, the dreaded harp comes round ;—
His turn is next.   Spell-bound poor Cœdmon sat
Amid his comrades.   They of beauty sang—
The peach that hangs on southern wall, so ripe,
So fragrant with God's breath, that it must cast
Its burden to the ground, was not more full,
Of luscious sweetness or of regal bloom
Than his o'erfreighted heart with beauty's sense.
Glory !—The mocking visions of his life,
One passionate out-pouring of his soul !
Had he not snatch'd a brand from nature's pyre,
Kindling thereby within his breast the flame,
Their song surpassing far, of holy love.
Oh ! for the rapturous word, the loosen'd tongue
To quell the heartache.   Should he try to break
This cruel spell that bound him ?   Not for him
The thrilling psalm of praise,—no, not for him
The heaven-born Allelnic chant to sing.
Ere the last stave of Haki's dirge was sung
Softly he glided from the board, and pass'd
With hasty steps into the wintry storm.
Homeward he turn'd, treading the frost-bound
          ground,
Stumbling along through lonely hidden ways,

Too full of misery to see or feel
The fleecy drift that silently enwrapp'd
The earth with stainless shroud.   The home-thatch
     gain'd,
He had the kine to fodder and to tend
(Day's tasks! sweet use of toil's necessity,
To staunch the flow from sorrow's unheal'd
     wounds.)
The welcome service done, free vent he gave
To the long pent-up grief of a vex'd life.
Hiding, upon a heap of straw he lay,
Darkening his soul with evil thoughts and gloom
Of uttermost despair.   Ah! drop by drop,
The cup had been fast filling; now the wave
Had leaped its margin, threatening in its flood
To drift away the strongholds of his faith,
His trust in God's sure mercy.   Henceforth life
Would be but barren waste; joy, beauty, cursed
By a felt blight of hopeless misery;
The pathways darken'd by vague, gloomy doubt,
Or haunted by pale ghosts of baffled hopes.

Despair hath many phases;—Vampire-like
It draws its vital essence from the soul,

Living by its undoing.   Like a dream
The past of many mercies is erased.
Quailing before a future drifts a soul
Shrouded in dark impenetrable gloom;—
To be !—a question of such misery,
So full of dull remorse and dead regrets,
That the frail life floats on, a waif, a stray,—
No good nor purpose in it.   The last drop
Distill'd from a long draught of bitterness
Poisons that hour.   Well if the All-Healer
With loving antidote sends angels forth
To strengthen feeble knees, lift the bow'd head,
And raise the eye to heaven.

                                  Cœdmon slept.—
A vision stood beside him.   One whose robe
Was dazzling brightness, as of sunlit snow
But newly strewn ; whose mien was majesty,
Whose brow was peace; a holy, pitying look
Deepened into a smile whilst gazing down
On the sleeper; then with voice, like melody
Of sweet bird thrilling on the peaceful dawn
Of spring's warm day, one hand uplifted, said,
" Cœdmon, arise and sing."

                                      Alas ! the woe,

The sorrow of his life!—" I cannot sing ! "
Again the voice : " Cœdmon, arise and sing ! "
" I cannot sing !   Have I not fled from friends,
Here hiding shame, because I cannot sing ?
What shall I sing ?   So do thou teach me then !
Full sure will I thy bidding do, and sing."
" Sing thy Creator's praise for his great love
To man ; how out of darkness He brought
          light ;
Order from out chaotic void and waste.
When seeing all things good how he placed man
To crown, and glorify his work.   Sing then
How from his high estate man sudden fell,
And leagued himself with evil—he, the creature
Made after God's own image.   Sing again
Of his redemption and his day of grace,
How love divine robed him in purity
Whereby to gain his lost pre-eminence !
Be this thy theme,—a song of praise to God
For highest, not for lowest gifts to man.
True words shall never fail thee—thou shalt
          learn
A song of such significance and power
The teaching shall outlast all lapse of time."

As on a summer's morn the dewy mists
Drift slowly upward, fading as they rise
In loftier currents, thus his vision died.
No need of actual sight to reassure
A doubting faith that holy visitant
Had stood beside him ; essence ambrosial
Had so impregn'd surrounding space with some
Exhaled virtue, that his spirit seem'd
Relumed, the while his limbs all listless fell
Enthrall'd by this new force.

                        Long stay'd he mazed,
Conning the teaching of that angel's song,
How God dwells not alone in circumstance
Of daily life and wondrous manifest
Of nature, but indwelling spirit here
With all humanity He lives in us,
And we through Him redeem'd and sanctified ;
His many attributes but vesture bright
Through which He makes earth with his beauty
      glad,
Yet only baser glory. Every throb
Of holiness, of purity, of love,
All noble deeds are loving witnesses
Of this indwelling spirit ever here

Shining throughout the world.

                      Not for man's praise,
Not for the gifts such things bring back to self;
Keep thy ways humble, pure, the rule of life
Was " Be ye holy, seeing I am so "
Thus sanctifying even life itself,
Standing before *him* not on special days
Or daily hours, but rendering worship due
In every inward thought and act of life.

  Oh ! for the means to sing the wondrous song
Unto his fellow men, imbibing thus
The strength and power that had imbued his soul
With holy transport.

                  With the morning came
Swift stir of active life and busy thought.
To his old friend the Reeve, Cœdmon resolved
To tell this vision of the night, and seek
His aid this loving message to make known.

  With finery of hoar-frost all the way
Was deck'd. Lace-work of various dainty webs
Netted the hedge-rows. Winter's magic touch
Had link'd sered leaves into bright coronals

And wreaths, laying them gently on the grave
Of the fast-dying year.   The drifted snow
High pinnacled form'd fitting canopies
Bright with prismatic colours.   Broken straws
Sparkling with crystals lay like runic lines
Of mighty meaning; 'tis with the mind's eye
The glinting emications we discern
Of a straw on biting winter's frozen track,
And broken emblem of unworthiness.

Greatly perplex'd the good Reeve heard
        throughout
Cœdmon's strange tale, which matter largely
        stretch'd
Beyond his compassing.   What did it mean?
What should a poor unletter'd carl like him
With visions do? His lonely moods were proof
Of mind bewilder'd, rather than high flights
Of holy inspiration;   such things came
To holy men through fastings oft, and great
Austerities.   Cœdmon was real and true,
And knowingly would never frame deceit
Whereby to snare a fellow-soul; but men
Were often trapp'd by self-conceit to sin

And vain delusions; thus he had great fear
Lest, by unholy influence possess'd,
His mind had lost its balance.   He would seek
From holy Lady Hilda clerkly aid
Ere yield a sanction to his friend's wild dream.

Forthwith he took his way toward the cliff
On which the abbey stood, and as he clomb
The hill-top many were his questionings
How best he could narrate this marvellous tale.
Admission gain'd, brief words of courtesy
And salutation, ere with fluent speech
He told his errand.   First of charity
He spoke, that fain would check this madman's
        hap;
Next, all men credulous and frail and yet
Some had a quicker insight into cause
Of slidings, could espy the bent of wrong,
While it escaped the facile sense, the slight
Unreasoning of others ; hence this great
Solicitude for Cædmon, dreamer, aye,
Through life full of conceits and strangest whims
With craving to excel in what to him
Seem'd God's wise purpose to withhold.   He fear'd

Lest this ambition had his judgment warp'd,
For never was he one of parts, or birth,
Or learning, nor aught knew he of past days
That could this strange assumption justify
Why miracle should be vouchsafed to him,
For miracle it must be or a snare
To lead him to perdition.   This the point
Whereon his judgment fail'd, and hers he sought.
With great experience best could she advise
Which way to act if for back-sliding son
A saintly remedy must be preferr'd,
Or did she think, forsooth, the dream divine,
How best to succour one so humbly born.

Long stay'd the abbess deep in prayerful thought,
Speaking at length.   " And who, my friend, shall say
What is a miracle ?   Our daily lives
Hanging on seeming chance, coming, the how
We know not ; going hence the same ! A day's
Brief span holds in its course the links
Of one continuous chain of miracles.
Each ear of ripen'd corn, or blade of grass,
Each flower unfolding scented petals bright

To the caressing sun, are miracles
So far beyond our ken and narrow grasp,
That we enjoy them with the air we breathe,
Taking no thought of a producing cause,
Each gift for our use coming yesterday,
To-day, to-morrow, being no marvels.
Yet are we blind, seeing, but seeing not,
If all the glorious mysteries abroad
Are only means for nourishing frail life,
Without that higher sense of homage felt
For the divinity that doth hedge us round.
How marvellous the miracles of thought,
That mystic clue inravelling all our deeds
With purposes of hidden good or ill !
Who can define these impulses of thought,
Know when the heart with inward yearning big
Throbs with that holier spirit, which would break
Through clinging trammels of humanity
That bind it to the world.   Our nobler self,
With nothing palpable or seen, it is
God's light in man, the soul quicken'd by breath
Of his voice calling.   Turn me the picture now.
Against such goodliness paint cold mistrust,
Envy, and jealous meanness, naming not

Sins broader, unassail'd from such like holding
Ourselves, that thus the whiteness of our souls
Be kept unstain'd.   Vain hope ! we chastise
The coarser daylight vices willingly,
Offending us in outward circumstance,
But the corroding taint of evil thought,
That like a leprosy enwraps our way,
Is for the eye of God alone to see.

The true, the beautiful, are only threads
Of purest gold, spun through the woof of life,
Albeit through coarsest grain of sin and ill.
Yet who shall say this act is evil all,
That one all good?   Give me not often here
Great mead of praise to actions that are bright
Only with glittering tinsel, having not
The golden thread of honest principle
For guarantee of worth, while many lives
Are wreck'd through wanton misuse of the gifts
Of nature's largess.   Prodigal out-flow
Fraying the virtue on the waste of life.
But let us hope that God will yet rebind
With his great love these torn and tatter'd threads,
Amidst his ransom'd jewels placing them

To shine with bright effulgence round his throne.
Not for us, then, these mysteries to solve;
They are the miracles that throng around
Our sojourn here.   No, my good, worthy Reeve,
Thus stands it with your friend.   We will not say
What you have stated to be true or false,
Bring the man hither.   Far as in us lies
We will essay to sift the truth, with God
On his behalf.   Nor will we of ourselves
Give judgment.   Saintly men shall yield us aid,
And your own council.   He shall sing his song,
If stays the gift with him.   If erring proved
Just admonition surely will accrue."

So on the given day there was great stir
And gathering without the abbey gates.
For Hilda's abbess claim'd a high descent;
Daughter and sister from a race of kings,
Her bidding was a law to all, the while
Hearts many she had won by kindly deeds,
By lovesome gifts and winning sympathy,
Making her life more holy than her words.
Within the abbey walls sat learned clerks
And holy monk from many a neighbouring cell

With Erlmen of great note.   High in the midst
The Lady abbess sat, and round her stood
White-veil'd and holy women bound to lead
A life of celibacy cold ; then came
The Reeve and Cœdmon, with a motley train
Of so-call'd friends ; those entry gain'd who could ;
The rest the issue stay'd without.   Cœdmon,
Like one half dead, scared by the thronging crowd,
The sea of upturn'd heads, the din, the glare,
Stood terror-stricken ; from his lifeless face
Utter disgrace was sure enough foretold,
With proof of wickedness and great deceit.
Gone was the rapture of triumphant faith
That throbb'd within his heart, blest consciousness
That God was with him ; sorrow and cold mistrust
Again enchain'd his words, and sent the thrill
Throughout his limbs as in days past.

                                        But, hark!
With clear sweet voice the abbess, rising, said,
" Cœdmon !   A tale of import marvellous
Of thee hath reach'd our ears !   How all thy life
Thou hast much yearn'd to sing, and never could'st ;
Now the gift given by angelic voice
Bidding thee sing !   A dream this sure must be

Or sad delusion, blinding all life's way
With the false glare of a deceiving hope.
Fain would we not believe falsehood could stain
Thy nature; yet deceits and frauds most strange
Are snares by which the evil one doth seek
To compass us in life, making pure truth
Seem falsehood, and a lie but holy truth.
Now by our calling we are bounden here
Truth to uphold with utmost diligence,
To test the same, from error freeing it.
On hearsay, then, this tale we cannot take.
God's dealings with his children while on earth
Must not be made a theme for mockery
Or wicked sport.   Thus we have thought it wise
To bid thee here, that we, assembled thus,
God helping us the while, should sift this truth,
Giving it holy sanction if deserved.
We hear thy song is pregnant with great thought,
And that thy words flow forth in harmony
Most winning to the sense.   Cædmon, we wait
The hearing of thy song, trusting all doubt
Will be removed, and grateful hearts give thanks
Will praise the giver of all good for this,
Thy heaven-born gift.   Cædmon! we thee await."

Was it his truth they question'd ? The vision
Of that long sad night, angel of his song,
But a base Godless lie ? Low bow'd his head,
Tightly his hands clasp'd, overpower'd by grief
And dead despair that flooded all his soul !
How to make good his words ? How give the
          proof
That holy visitant beside him then
Had stood and taught him things divine ? He
          lifts
His eyes.   Behold ! the Angel in the midst,
The same sweet voice thrilling upon his sense—
" Fear nothing, do my bidding, rise and sing."
Ah ! the bright radiancy from upturn'd eyes,
The calm seraphic smile that lit the face,
As with unfolded hands he raised his voice
And sang his song.   *   *   *   *
          *   *   *   It were too long, too long,
Here to repeat his wondrous tale.   Enough
To give the prayer by which, commencing, first
He ask'd for help and guidance from above ;
The teaching lives with us, as truly here
The spirit's sustenance and vital strength,
As the pure air health to the mortal frame.

" Teach me, Almighty God ! for I have learn'd
Without Thee, helpless, poor, I nothing am,
With measureless persuasive mercy; Thou
Ever art leading on through unseen paths
Thy erring children, willing not that one
Should perish; lovingly Thou tendest him
That, frail, slips from the right, while wayward
    wand'rings
Become, like clinging ivy, stronger stays
To grasp the love upholding him on earth.
Indwelling spirit ! in this hour of need,
Help me ! unseal my blind and darken'd sight,
And teach me Thee to see.   In all Thy ways
Most wonderful art Thou, and I have traced
Thy loving footsteps on this gladsome earth
In winter's snow-flakes, in the summer's beam,
In the young spring's first blush, in the last sigh
Of dying autumn; in the slow, long flight
Of querulous and sable-mated rook,
As in the midge's day-dream ; in the flash
Of riven fire, hurl'd with loud thunder-clap ;
In dripping rain, or mid uprooting wind
That telleth not from whither it hath come
Or whither gone.   Things beauteous with Thy life

Have been my pastime.   There are footsteps yet
Where I would follow.   Lead, oh! lead me then
To learn Thy higher mercies unto man!
How to approach Thee, Lord, yet I know not;
But call Thou me, and I shall hear Thy voice!
If they who seek Thee here find truth, grant me
That truth.   If wisdom, give me, then, that gift.
If love, shed Thou that love on me.   The sun
Sheddeth its light on many stars! On me
Shed Thou the glory of Thy love, and make
Me render back that light; and lower mists
Will never dim the faith illumined thus
By Thy supreme effulgence."   *   *

          *   *   *   *   *

          *   *   *   *.   *

Hush'd was the voice of Cœdmon; Silence deep
Fill'd the wide hall ; eyes, moist with unshed tears
Were gazing on him ; lips apart, waiting
Some further words expectant stay'd.   At length
Murmur of bated passing whispers rose,
Which, onward rolling, gathered strength, until
One strain of loud triumphant gladness rang
From the dense crowd.   As the sound died away,
The abbess, standing up, 'midst silence, said:

" Cœdmon ! beloved of God !   Thee we arise
To greet, believing thou art taught of Him ;
That are we all, but He at times doth choose
To set some vessel higher than the rest,
And fill it with His glory, outward sign
Significant of this high calling here ;
There being none, He knowing well the while,
From out His seed broad-cast upon the earth
When best to reap the full-ear'd corn ; wheat-
    sheaf
Fullest reward for toil will render back
And culture given.   Thee hath He chosen thus
A beacon-light to guide life's mariners
Upon their way, shining athwart the mists
Of ignorance and sin.   Come now with us
As means of working out His high behests,
And sanctuary take within these walls.
Those versed in ancient lore shall re-translate
Pages of Holy Writ which thou shalt frame
Into sweet songs and loving-sounding rhymes
In thine own Saxon tongue ; and they shall be
The first flow of a stream that knows no ebb,
Whose waters shall to all men healing give,
Bearing upon its flood the desolate,

The broken-hearted, till they reach the sea
Which passeth this life to Eternity ! ''

  So Cœdmon lived and died a holy monk
At Stronesleigh; and heathen hands despoil'd
The sacred fane with ruthless ruin.—Time
'Neath his green sward one part hath buried deep,
And changes many since have swept the land,
Changes as of fast-fleeting day and night
When rim of dawn first stirs the quivering veil
Of darkness, though the bright morning-star
Yet queens it high against the rising sun ;
Changes of shadow and soft mountain lights,
Of the wild storm that roughly rends away
Its beauty's strength, until its fragments piled
In broken grandeur rear its cenotaph.
Type of the hope that grows beneath the noon's
Warm breath, but like an infant's day just
      breathes
Upon the world, and smiling leaves the heart
In darkness; changes as of faltering steps
From childish feet, unto the shuffling gait
Of tottering age.   But midst this ceaseless round
Of death in life and life in death (for death

In nature is but other birth rising
To fuller life), one thing alone remains
Unchanging; 'tis the love that would not break
The bruised reed, first taught in Cœdmon's song.
The rustling grass comes up, and withering dies,
The fairest flower that blooms fades on its stem,
But *His Word*, like the Everlasting Hills,
Will stand through generations yet unborn,
The highest glory when the trumpet's sound
Shall give that certain sound "Time is no more."

CHISWICK PRESS :—PRINTED BY WHITTINGHAM AND WILKINS,
TOOKS COURT, CHANCERY LANE.